Built for Speed

The World's Fastest Stock Cars

by Jeff Savage

CAPSTONE
HIGH-INTEREST
BOOKS

an imprint of Capstone Press
Mankato, Minnesota

Capstone High-Interest Books are published by Capstone Press
151 Good Counsel Drive, P.O. Box 669, Mankato, Minnesota 56002.
http://www.capstone-press.com

Library of Congress Cataloging-in-Publication Data
Savage, Jeff, 1961–
    The world's fastest stock cars/by Jeff Savage.
    p. cm.—(Built for speed)
    Summary: Examines the history, design, safety features, and professional
racing of stock cars.
    Includes bibliographical references and index.
    ISBN 0-7368-1503-1 (hardcover)
    1. Stock cars (Automobiles)—Juvenile literature. [1. Stock cars
(Automobiles) 2. Stock car racing.] I. Title. II. Built for speed (Mankato,
Minn.) III. Series.
TL236.28 .S28 2003
796.72—dc21   2002012649

**Capstone Press thanks Curtis Hogan and NASCAR's Public Relations
department for their help in preparing this book.**

Editorial Credits
Matt Doeden, editor; Karen Risch, product planning editor; Timothy Halldin,
series designer; Patrick D. Dentinger, book designer; Jo Miller, photo researcher

Photo Credits
Corbis/Bettmann, 10, 12
Getty Images/Donald Miralle, 8; Chris Stanford, 16, 20; Robert Laberge, 30;
    Doug Pensinger, 33; Jonathan Ferrey, cover, 38, 43
SportsChrome-USA, 24; Brian Spurlock, 4, 7, 14, 28–29; Greg Crisp, 19, 23,
    26, 34, 37, 40

1 2 3 4 5 6 08 07 06 05 04 03

Table of Contents

Chapter 1

Stock Cars

Forty-three stock cars line up in two rows on the grid behind the starting line. The drivers keep their cars in line as they follow the pace car once around the oval track. The flagman waves a green flag to start the race.

The powerful cars roar around the first turn at more than 100 miles (160 kilometers) per hour. The smell of exhaust and burning rubber from skidding tires fills the air. The drivers complete the first turn and speed down the backstretch at almost 200 miles (320 kilometers) per hour.

Drivers step on and off the throttle as they try to pass one another. Thirty laps later, two

Drivers form two long rows at the beginning of each race.

cars accidentally bump. One of the cars crashes into the concrete wall that surrounds the track. The car is badly damaged and cannot finish the race. The flagman waves a yellow flag to tell other drivers to slow down. Emergency crews rush onto the track to remove the car and to make sure the driver is all right.

The drivers make a pit stop for more fuel and new tires. They then return to the track to continue the race. They still have 170 laps to go.

About Stock Cars

Stock cars are high-performance racing vehicles that are based on the design of standard road cars. All stock cars are two-door coupes. Four companies build professional stock cars. The companies are Chevrolet, Ford, Dodge, and Pontiac.

Stock car racing is very expensive. Each car frame costs about $70,000. Each engine costs

All stock cars are two-door coupes.

about $35,000. Racing teams must replace the engine after each race. Racing teams also spend thousands of dollars each race on tires and fuel.

NASCAR teams earn money through sponsorships and race prizes. Sponsors pay racing teams to promote products. For example, a tire company may pay a team to display the company's logo on the hood of a racecar. Teams also receive prize money for racing. The biggest stock car races are in the NASCAR Winston Cup Series. Each Winston Cup race pays out hundreds of thousands of dollars in prize money. Much of this money goes to the top finishers, but all of the teams in the race receive some money.

Sponsors pay racing teams to display company logos on cars.

Chapter 2

The History of Stock Cars

Stock car racing began in the southern United States during the 1920s. During this time, a U.S. law made the sale of alcohol illegal. Some people made and sold alcohol anyway. They sometimes changed their cars so they could outrun law enforcement officials. People often called these cars "runner cars."

Drivers began to race their runner cars on dirt roads. Soon, people built tracks just for racing. People sometimes paid to see the races. Winning drivers received some of the money collected from the fans.

Stock car racing's popularity grew during the 1950s.

NASCAR set rules that made all of the cars in a race about equal.

The Birth of NASCAR

Stock car racing became more popular in the South during the 1930s and early 1940s. Each racetrack had its own rules. The different sets of rules often confused drivers and fans.

In 1947, a driver and race promoter named Bill France arranged a meeting at a hotel in

Daytona Beach, Florida. France invited 35 other drivers and race promoters. The group created an organization to govern all stock car races in the United States. The rules would be the same at every track. France named the organization the National Association for Stock Car Auto Racing. He called it NASCAR for short.

NASCAR's main race group was called the Strictly Stock Division. In this racing class, drivers could not make changes to a car's frame or body. They could only change the engine. They also could make certain changes inside the car for safety reasons. The Strictly Stock Division later grew into the kind of stock car racing popular today.

The Growth of NASCAR
NASCAR helped the sport of stock car racing grow. More fans went to races. Drivers improved their skills and their cars. Soon, carmakers wanted to build cars specifically for the sport. They believed that having their cars win races would be good for business.

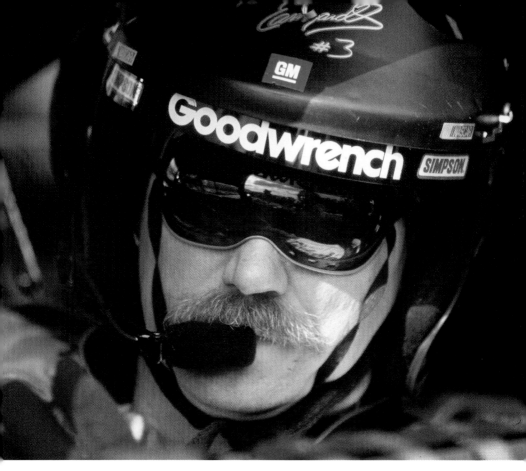

Dale Earnhardt was one of NASCAR's most popular drivers during the 1990s.

Stock car races became popular across the United States in the 1960s and 1970s. More paved racetracks were built. TV networks broadcast NASCAR races. David Pearson, Richard Petty, and other successful drivers became racing stars.

Racing Today

Stock car racing grew in popularity again during the late 1990s and early 2000s. Jeff Gordon, Dale Earnhardt, Bobby Labonte, and other top drivers helped to increase interest in the sport.

Today, stock car racing is one of the biggest sports in North America. Crowds of 100,000 fans or more are common at many Winston Cup events. Millions more fans watch the races on TV. Drivers can earn millions of dollars in prize money and sponsorships.

Stock car racing is most popular in the United States, but Canada also has stock car races. In 1981, the Canadian Association for Stock Car Auto Racing (CASCAR) was formed. CASCAR races are similar to NASCAR races. But the highest level of stock car racing competition still takes place in NASCAR's Winston Cup Series.

Chapter 3

Stock Car Design

Today's stock cars are highly modified versions of standard cars. Drivers can use one of four U.S. car models in NASCAR races. The models are the Chevrolet Monte Carlo, the Dodge Intrepid, the Ford Taurus, and the Pontiac Grand Prix. These four models are all about equal in performance.

Racing teams start with the basic body design of each car. They strip out unneeded parts such as passenger seats. They add roll bars and other safety features. They then add high-powered engines to prepare the cars for racing.

The Ford Taurus is one of four car models used in NASCAR races.

Engines

The engine is the most important change teams make to a stock car. Stock cars have internal combustion engines. These engines burn fuel inside a set of cylinders. The burning causes pistons inside the cylinders to pump up and down quickly. This motion powers the car.

Stock car engines have eight cylinders arranged in the shape of a letter "V." They are often called V-8 engines. These powerful engines can produce more than 700 horsepower. Standard car engines produce about 150 horsepower.

Stock car engines burn fuel more quickly than standard engines do. A stock car can travel only about 5 miles (8 kilometers) for each gallon of fuel it burns. Stock cars must have large fuel tanks to make up for poor fuel mileage.

Racing teams usually use a new engine for each race. After the race, the team removes the main body of the engine, called the block.

Stock car engines can produce more than 700 horsepower.

Mechanics build a new engine around the block. Top racing teams can spend $1 million or more per year on engines.

In the past, many racing teams used several engines each week. They used one engine for practice, a new engine for qualifying laps, and another engine for the race. In 2002, NASCAR added a rule to reduce the number of engines

that race teams use in a week. The rule forces any team that changes its engine after qualifying to start the race at the rear of the starting grid.

The Body

The main body of a stock car is called the chassis. All of the car's other parts, including the wheels and the frame, connect to the chassis. The frame includes the panels that surround the car.

Race teams work to reduce air resistance, or drag, on their stock cars. Drag slows down moving objects. Teams use the science of aerodynamics to build cars with little drag. Aerodynamic designs help stock cars reach speeds of more than 200 miles (320 kilometers) per hour.

Stock cars have a strip of metal called a spoiler attached to the rear of the chassis. The spoiler is shaped so that passing air pushes down on the car. This air pressure,

The main body of a stock car is called the chassis.

called downforce, helps the car's rear tires grip the track. Downforce makes the car more stable at high speeds. Racing teams carefully adjust the spoiler before a race. The car could spin if it does not have enough downforce. If it has too much downforce, the car will be too slow.

Tires and Brakes

Stock cars use soft, smooth tires called slicks. These tires grip smooth track surfaces easily, but they also wear down quickly. For this reason, race teams must change the tires several times during a race.

Race teams often use different styles of tires on the right side of the car than they do on the left side. They do this because many tracks are ovals, and cars only have to turn left. The right-side tires are sometimes called the outside tires because they always face away from the center of the track. The outside tires are often slightly larger than the inside tires.

Every stock car has a spoiler attached to the rear of the chassis.

The air pressure inside the tires may also be different. Race teams adjust the tires until the car is well balanced. They closely watch the tires during a race. They tell the driver to make a pit stop when the tires begin to wear.

Stock car brakes are similar to those in a standard car. The brake connects to brake pads on the wheels. The brake pads squeeze against the wheels to slow down the car.

Stock car drivers frequently use their brakes. They often drive less than 12 inches (30 centimeters) behind the car in front of them. This strategy is called drafting. Cars can reach higher speeds and get better fuel mileage while drafting. But drivers also need strong, dependable brakes to avoid bumping into each other.

Smooth tires called slicks give stock cars a good grip on paved tracks.

Chapter 4

Stock Car Races

Racing teams carefully adjust their cars each week for the upcoming race. Drivers study the racetrack. They try to learn how fast they can go as they enter turns. Crew chiefs develop a racing plan for the team. They decide how many pit stops the driver will need and how aggressive the driver should be in passing other cars.

Tracks

The three main types of stock car racetracks are superspeedways, short tracks, and road courses. Superspeedways are large oval-shaped tracks with banked turns. Banked

Martinsville and other short tracks have sharp curves and short straightaways.

turns are sloped inward toward the center of the track. Banking helps cars turn easily without skidding off the track. Cars often travel at 200 miles (320 kilometers) per hour or faster on superspeedways.

Short tracks are less than 1 mile (1.6 kilometers) long. Most short tracks are oval shaped. They usually have tight

Cars can reach speeds of more than 200 miles (320 kilometers) per hour on superspeedways.

turns that force drivers to use their brakes. Turns may have slight banking or no banking. Drivers must drive more slowly on short tracks. On some tracks, their average speeds are slower than 100 miles (160 kilometers) per hour.

A road course is a paved track with many turns. Road courses have many features that oval-shaped tracks do not. Drivers must make turns both to the left and to the right. Some road courses have tight hairpin turns. These sharp turns often force drivers to slow down to 50 miles (80 kilometers) per hour or less. Road courses also may have hills.

Events

Most stock car races are grouped into series. Each series includes a set number of races. Drivers earn series points depending on their finish in each race. The driver with the most points at the end of the season wins the series.

Drivers can take part in a variety of series. Some series include races in one region. For example, the Raybestos Northwest Series is a series of races that take place in northwestern states such as Washington, Montana, and Idaho. Other series include races from all over the United States or Canada. NASCAR's

NASCAR's Winston Cup Series is the most popular group of stock car races.

Busch Series and Winston Cup Series are among the most popular racing series.

The Winston Cup Series begins each February with the Daytona 500 at the Daytona International Speedway in Florida. Many racing fans consider the Daytona 500 to be the most important stock car race in the world. Other famous races include the Brickyard 400 at the Indianapolis Motor Speedway in Indiana and the Virginia 500 at Martinsville Speedway.

Before the Race

The first step in taking part in a stock car race is qualifying. Each driver must make a qualifying run to decide the starting order of the race. These runs are also called time trials. Only one driver at a time takes part in a time trial. Race officials measure each driver's lap times.

The driver with the fastest lap begins the race in first place, which is called the pole position. The rest of the drivers line up on the starting grid based on their qualifying times.

The pole position is the inside car on the front row.

The second-place driver starts on the outside position of the first row. The other cars line up behind these two cars.

Only 43 cars can take part in a stock car race. Time trials determine most of these cars. Most series races set aside a few extra spots. Drivers who are high in the series point standings can use one of these provisional spots if they have a bad time trial. This rule allows race officials to make sure the most popular drivers will be able to race. Provisional drivers start the race at the back of the starting grid.

Before the race, NASCAR officials inspect every car. They make sure each car is built according to the sport's rules. For example, a car's fuel tank can hold no more than 22 gallons (83 liters) of fuel.

Pit Stops

Some stock car races are as long as 600 miles (966 kilometers). Drivers must make many stops in the pit area for fuel and new tires.

NASCAR officials inspect each car before a race.

Each race team has a small space in the pit area to make adjustments to their car. This space is called the pit box.

A race team must have a good pit crew to win a race. The pit crew is a team of six skilled mechanics and specialists who make sure the car performs well. They wait near the team's pit box.

Each time the driver makes a pit stop, the pit crew rushes into the pit box. One member uses a jack to lift up one side of the car. Other members change the tires on that side. They then move to the other side of the car. At the same time, other pit crew members pour fuel into the fuel tank, wash the windows, give the driver a drink, and make any other adjustments needed. They then help push the car out of the pit box as the driver heads back onto the track. All of these tasks take only about 15 seconds.

During a pit stop, pit crews change tires, add gas, and make other needed repairs.

Chapter 5

Stock Car Stars

As the popularity of stock car racing has grown, the sport's top drivers have become more famous. David Pearson and Richard Petty were among the earliest NASCAR stars. Today's racing stars include Dale Earnhardt Jr., Jeff Gordon, and Tony Stewart.

Dale Earnhardt Jr.

Dale Earnhardt Jr. comes from a family of stock car drivers. His father, Dale Earnhardt Sr., was one of the most successful drivers in NASCAR history. Earnhardt Sr. died in a crash in the 2001 Daytona 500. Dale's brother, Kerry, races in NASCAR's Busch Series.

Earnhardt Jr. started his racing career at age 17 at a track in his hometown of Concord,

Dale Earnhardt Jr. started his Winston Cup career in 2000.

North Carolina. He began his NASCAR career in the Busch Series, where he won the championship in 1998. In 2000, Earnhardt moved up to the Winston Cup Series. He won two races in his first season and finished second in points among rookie drivers. In 2001, he won three races and finished eighth in the Winston Cup point standings.

Jeff Gordon

Jeff Gordon is NASCAR's biggest star and one of the most successful drivers in the history of stock car racing. He began his racing career at age 5 when he raced small vehicles called quarter midgets.

Gordon started his NASCAR career in 1992 in the Busch Series. In 1993, he moved to the Winston Cup Series and was named Rookie of the Year. Gordon won the Winston Cup title in 1995, 1997, 1998, and 2001. In 1998, he became only the third driver in Winston Cup history to win four races in a row.

Jeff Gordon was the most successful NASCAR driver of the 1990s and early 2000s.

Tony Stewart

Many NASCAR experts agree that Tony Stewart is the best road course driver in NASCAR. He is also among the best short track drivers.

Stewart learned to race by driving go-karts and other small vehicles. As a teenager, Stewart raced as often as he could. He quickly showed that he could win with almost any kind of vehicle and on any kind of track. In the late 1990s, he was a champion Indy car driver. He immediately became a star when he started driving in the Winston Cup Series in 1999. He won three races in his first year and was named Rookie of the Year.

Stewart continued to improve after his rookie season. In 2000, he won six races and finished sixth in the Winston Cup point standings. In 2001, he finished second in the point standings.

Tony Stewart is a skilled Indy car driver as well as a stock car driver.

Words to Know

aerodynamic (air-oh-dye-NAM-mik)—designed to reduce air resistance

chassis (CHASS-ee)—the frame on which the body of a stock car is mounted

cylinder (SIL-uhn-dur)—a hollow tube inside which a piston moves up and down to generate power in an engine

drafting (DRAF-ting)—a strategy in which a driver closely follows another car to reduce air resistance

modify (MOD-uh-fye)—to change; mechanics modify the engine and body of a stock car to improve its performance.

slicks (SLIKS)—soft tires that have no tread

spoiler (SPOI-lur)—a winglike device attached to the back of a stock car; spoilers help a stock car's rear tires grip the track.

traction (TRAK-shuhn)—the grip of a stock car's tires on the ground

To Learn More

Cefrey, Holly. *Stock Car.* Built for Speed. New York: Children's Press, 2001.

Dubois, Muriel L. *Pro Stock Cars.* Wild Rides! Mankato, Minn.: Capstone Press, 2002.

Johnstone, Michael. *NASCAR.* The Need for Speed. Minneapolis: LernerSports, 2002.

Stewart, Mark. *Daytona 500.* The Watts History of Sports. New York: Franklin Watts, 2002.

Useful Addresses

CASCAR
9763 Glendon Drive
Komoka, ON N0L 1R0
Canada

**Daytona International Speedway
  Visitors Center**
1801 West International Speedway Boulevard
Daytona Beach, FL 32114

Indianapolis Motor Speedway
4790 West 16th Street
Indianapolis, IN 46222

NASCAR
P.O. Box 2875
Daytona Beach, FL 32120

Internet Sites

Do you want to learn more about stock cars?
Visit the FACT HOUND at *http://www.facthound.com*

FACT HOUND can track down many sites to help you.
All the FACT HOUND sites are hand-selected by Capstone
Press editors. FACT HOUND will fetch the best, most accurate
information to answer your questions.

IT IS EASY! IT IS FUN!
1) Go to *http://www.facthound.com*
2) Type in: 0736815031
3) Click on "FETCH IT" and FACT HOUND will put you on
the trail of several helpful links.

**You can also search by subject or book title. So, relax
and let our pal FACT HOUND do the research for you!**

Index